THE UNTOLD HISTORY
OF ANCIENT CIVILIZATIONS

AZTECS

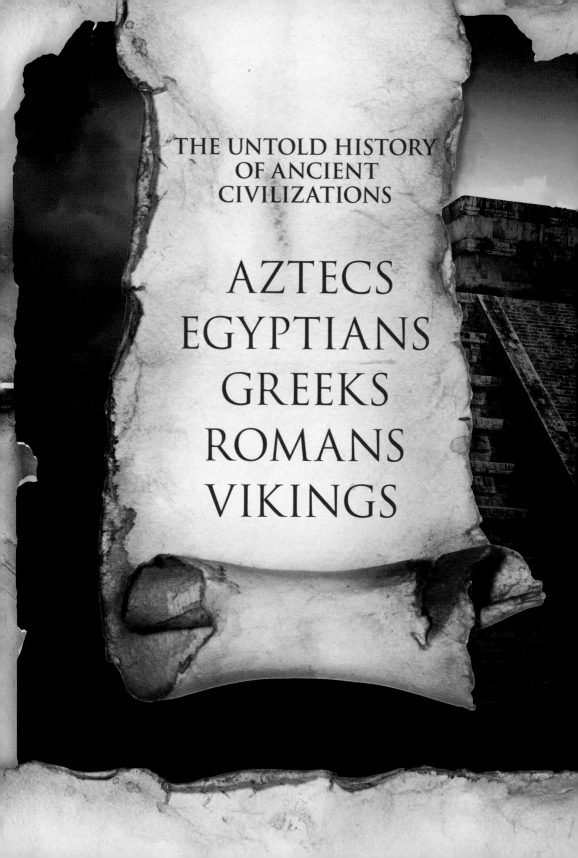

THE UNTOLD HISTORY
OF ANCIENT
CIVILIZATIONS

AZTECS
EGYPTIANS
GREEKS
ROMANS
VIKINGS

THE UNTOLD HISTORY
OF ANCIENT CIVILIZATIONS

AZTECS

MASON CREST
PHILADELPHIA
MIAMI

Mason Crest
450 Parkway Drive, Suite D
Broomall, Pennsylvania 19008
(866) MCP-BOOK (toll-free)
www.masoncrest.com

ISBN (hardback) 978-1-4222-3518-8
ISBN (series) 978-1-4222-3517-1
ISBN (ebook) 978-1-4222-8338-7

Cataloging-in-Publication Data on file with the Library of Congress

NATIONAL
HIGHLIGHTS

Developed and produced by Mason Crest
Editor: Keri DeDeo
Interior and cover design: Jana Rade
Production: Michelle Luke

QR CODES AND LINKS TO THIRD-PARTY CONTENT
You may gain access to certain third-party content ("Third-Party Sites") by scanning and using the QR Codes that appear in this publication (the "QR Codes"). We do not operate or control in any respect any information, products, or services on such Third-Party Sites linked to by us via the QR Codes included in this publication, and we assume no responsibility for any materials you may access using the QR Codes. Your use of the QR Codes may be subject to terms, limitations, or restrictions set forth in the applicable terms of use or otherwise established by the owners of the Third-Party Sites. Our linking to such Third-Party Sites via the QR Codes does not imply an endorsement or sponsorship of such Third-Party Sites or the information, products, or services offered on or through the Third-Party Sites, nor does it imply an endorsement or sponsorship of this publication by the owners of such Third-Party Sites.

CONTENTS

KEY ICONS TO LOOK FOR:

 WORDS TO UNDERSTAND: These words with their easy-to-understand definitions will increase the reader's understanding of the text while building vocabulary skills.

 SIDEBARS: This boxed material within the main text allows readers to build knowledge, gain insights, explore possibilities, and broaden their perspectives by weaving together additional information to provide realistic and holistic perspectives.

 EDUCATIONAL VIDEOS: Readers can view videos by scanning our QR codes, providing them with additional educational content to supplement the text. Examples include news coverage, moments in history, speeches, iconic sports moments, and much more!

 TEXT-DEPENDENT QUESTIONS: These questions send the reader back to the text for more careful attention to the evidence presented there.

 RESEARCH PROJECTS: Readers are pointed toward areas of further inquiry connected to each chapter. Suggestions are provided for projects that encourage deeper research and analysis.

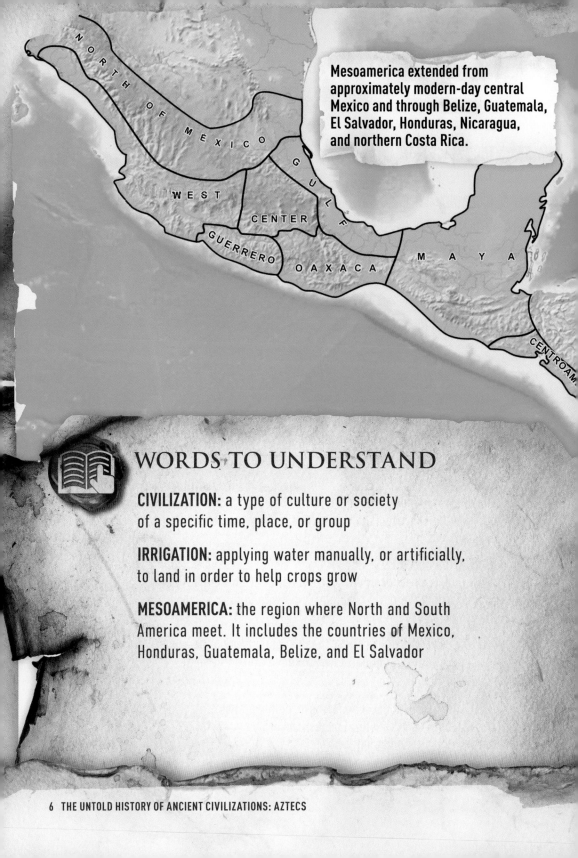

Mesoamerica extended from approximately modern-day central Mexico and through Belize, Guatemala, El Salvador, Honduras, Nicaragua, and northern Costa Rica.

NORTH OF MEXICO

WEST

GULF

CENTER

GUERRERO

OAXACA

MAYA

CENTROAM.

WORDS TO UNDERSTAND

CIVILIZATION: a type of culture or society of a specific time, place, or group

IRRIGATION: applying water manually, or artificially, to land in order to help crops grow

MESOAMERICA: the region where North and South America meet. It includes the countries of Mexico, Honduras, Guatemala, Belize, and El Salvador

CHAPTER 1

THE AZTECS MOVE IN

A round 1200 AD, small European nations were struggling to survive during the Middle Ages. But in **Mesoamerica**, the Aztecs were poised to take over the entire region—more than 80,000 sq. mi. (130,000 sq. km).

Originally, the Aztec people lived in North America in Aztlan, or the White Land. They were farmers and warriors. But, mysteriously, they left their homeland. This may have been because of climate change. Probably, the Aztecs ran short of water, and their crops died. So, led by priests carrying a statue of their tribal god Huitzilopochtli (say "hweet-sil-oh-pok-tlee"), they headed south, looking for a new home. They were on the move for about 200 years.

When the Aztecs arrived in Mesoamerica, they found it was already very full! For more than 2,000 years, the region had been home to many splendid **civilizations**, including the Olmecs, the Maya, and the

Examine the Aztecs' impressive system of aqueducts that supplied water for irrigation and bathing.

This illustration depicts Huitzilopochtli, the Aztec god of sun.

Toltecs. Many smaller groups of people also lived there. Each civilization had its own language, laws, customs, and skills, but they also shared many traditions.

This ancient city of Maya was uncovered in Palenque, Chiapas, Mexico. The Maya was just one civilization the Aztecs found when they arrived in Mesoamerica.

The Aztecs were crafty and clever. They quickly learned what they could from Mesoamerican peoples but kept all their own ancient laws and customs as well. This meant they had lots of wisdom, knowledge, and practical experience to help them to survive. They were experts at farming and even used **irrigation**.

The name of Mexico comes from the word "Mexica," which is what the Aztecs called themselves in their native language of Nahuatl.

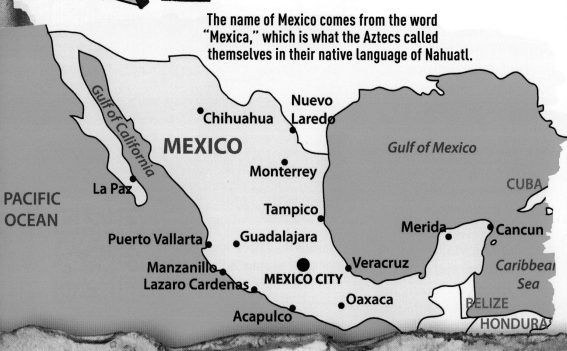

PACIFIC OCEAN

Gulf of California

MEXICO

Chihuahua

Nuevo Laredo

Gulf of Mexico

CUBA

Monterrey

La Paz

Tampico

Merida

Cancun

Puerto Vallarta

Guadalajara

Veracruz

Caribbean Sea

Manzanillo

Lazaro Cardenas

MEXICO CITY

Oaxaca

BELIZE

Acapulco

HONDURAS

This ancient city of Maya was uncovered in Palenque, Chiapas, Mexico. The Maya was just one civilization the Aztecs found when they arrived in Mesoamerica.

SAY IT IN AZTEC

The Aztecs spoke *Nahuatl* (say "nah-hwatull"). It was related to several Native North American languages and quite different from most others spoken in the land where they settled. In Nahuatl, the Aztecs' name for themselves was "Mexica" (say "mesh-ee-ca"). Today, this has become the name of a nation, Mexico. And more than 2 million native Mexicans speak Nahuatl today.

TEXT-DEPENDENT QUESTIONS

1. What modern countries make up ancient Mesoamerica?
2. When the Aztecs arrived in Mesoamerica, they found many people already there. Name three of these civilizations the Aztecs found.
3. What expertise did the Aztecs have that helped them survive in such inhospitable surroundings?

RESEARCH PROJECT

The Aztecs used irrigation to water their crops, but they did not have sprinklers like we do today. Research how the Aztecs and other ancient civilizations used irrigation to water their crops. Write a two- to three-page report explaining what you found. Ask your teacher if you can show your class what you discovered.

The prickly pear cactus was found everywhere in the Aztecs' new home.

WORDS TO UNDERSTAND

ARCHITECT: a person who designs buildings and other structures

DROUGHT: when there is not enough water to provide for people, animals, and crops

POISONOUS: something that is dangerous or destructive; some plants and animals can be dangerous to humans and animals

CHAPTER 2

THE DREAM CITY

The Aztecs were not welcomed with open arms when they arrived on the scene. But they needed a new home and weren't about to turn around. They believed they were working from a message from their god. They were to build a city where they saw an eagle eating a snake, sitting in a prickly pear cactus.

So they traveled searching for the dream sign. Finally they found it, around AD 1325. But it was on a barren island, crawling with snakes, in the middle of a swampy lake in the deep Central Valley of Mexico. Close by, volcanoes released clouds of **poisonous** gas. Powerful tribes lived all around the area. How could anyone make a home there?

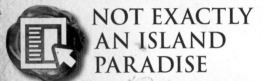

NOT EXACTLY AN ISLAND PARADISE

The Aztecs' city was not a healthy place to live. Its climate was harsh, with **droughts** and heat waves. There were also poisonous plants and spiders and the threat of earthquakes. Killer germs and mosquitoes bred in the lake, which slowly grew salty and slimy as its water evaporated.

How did the Aztecs survive in such a hostile place? One thing that helped was that they used everything they had—even human waste, which they used to fertilize their farms and tan leather.

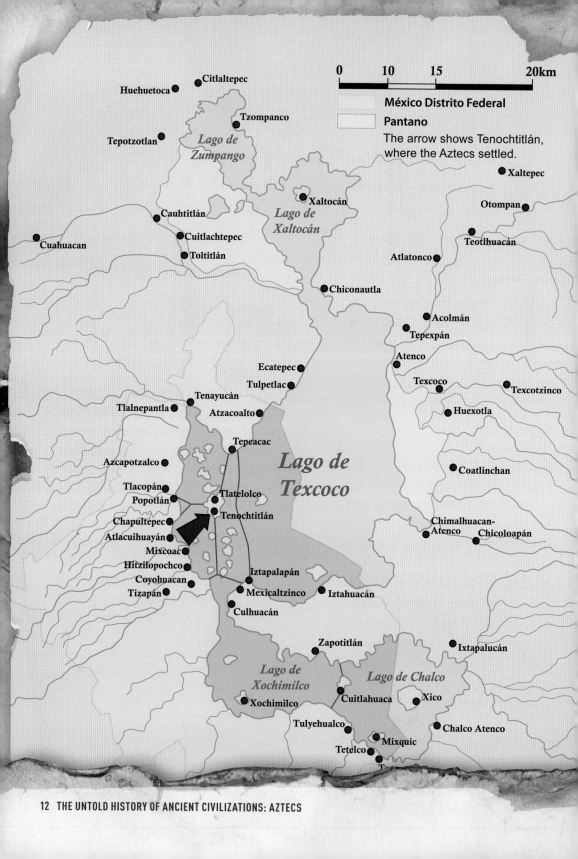

Huehuetoca

Citlaltepec

Tzompanco

Tepotzotlan

Lago de Zumpango

Cuauhuacan

Cauhtitlán

Cuitlachtepec

Toltitlán

Xaltocán

Lago de Xaltocán

Chiconautla

Xaltepec

Otompan

Teotíhuacán

Atlatonco

Acolmán

Tepexpán

Atenco

Texcoco

Texcotzinco

Ecatepec

Tulpetlac

Tenayucán

Atzacoalto

Huexotla

Tlalnepantla

Tepeacac

Lago de Texcoco

Azcapotzalco

Coatlinchan

Tlacopán

Popotlán

Tlatelolco

Tenochtitlán

Chapúltepec

Atlacuihuayán

Chimalhuacan-Atenco

Chicoloapán

Mixcoac

Hítzilopochco

Coyohuacan

Iztapalapán

Tizapán

Mexicaltzinco

Iztahuacán

Culhuacán

Zapotitlán

Ixtapalucán

Lago de Xochimilco

Lago de Chalco

Xochimilco

Cuitlahuaca

Xico

Tulyehualco

Chalco Atenco

Tetelco

Mixquic

0   10   15   20km

México Distrito Federal

Pantano

The arrow shows Tenochtitlán, where the Aztecs settled.

The Aztecs were sure they would survive. To them, this unpromising site was the center of the universe, and Aztec people were brave as well as determined. They killed the snakes and ate them and built houses and temples on the island. They gave their city a name, Tenochtitlán (say "tay-nok-teet-lan"), which means "place of the prickly pear." There was no space on the island to grow food, so Aztec farmers built *chinampas* (say "chee-nam-pas"), or floating farms, all around it in the lake. The created friendships with their neighbors to avoid conflicts—at least at first.

Aztec **architects** designed a huge aqueduct to bring fresh water to the city from mountain streams and built raised walkways across the shallow lake. These linked the island to the surrounding shore. By 1500, Tenochtitlán was one of the biggest cities in the world.

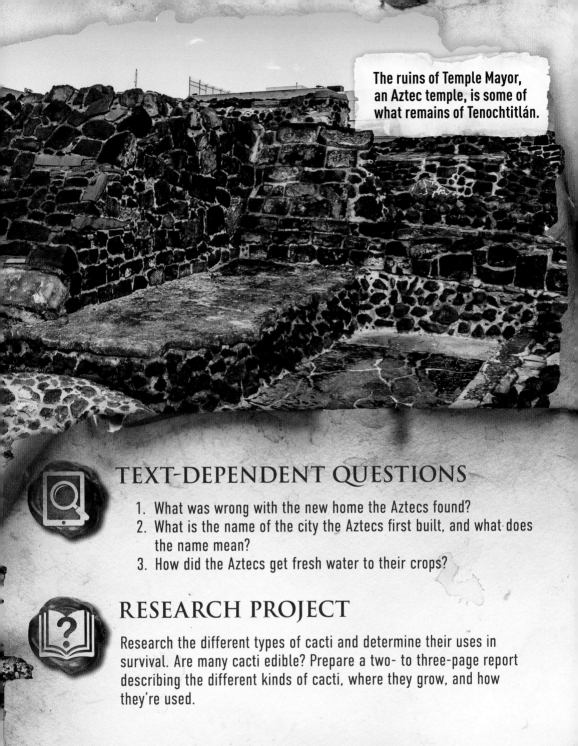

The ruins of Temple Mayor, an Aztec temple, is some of what remains of Tenochtitlán.

TEXT-DEPENDENT QUESTIONS

1. What was wrong with the new home the Aztecs found?
2. What is the name of the city the Aztecs first built, and what does the name mean?
3. How did the Aztecs get fresh water to their crops?

RESEARCH PROJECT

Research the different types of cacti and determine their uses in survival. Are many cacti edible? Prepare a two- to three-page report describing the different kinds of cacti, where they grow, and how they're used.

This monument in Veracruz, Mexico is of the last known Mexica ruler (Tlatoani), Cuauhtemoc.

WORDS TO UNDERSTAND

KINGSHIP: a form of government that is ruled by a king rather than an elected official

PUNISHMENT: a penalty that is applied when someone breaks a rule or law

SCRIBE: a person who serves as a writer or copier; before the invention of printing, scribes handwrote copies of manuscripts

CHAPTER 3

HIGH AND MIGHTY

A t first, the Aztecs were led by the Great Speaker, or Tlatoani (say "tlah-twa-nee"), who was elected. He had a deputy named Snake Woman, or Cihuacoatl (say "si-hwa-ko-at-ull"). The Aztecs weren't ahead of their time, though, as Snake Woman was always a man. After a while, a single family took over the position of Great Speaker, and then it was passed, like a **kingship**, from father to son.

The Great Speaker did business from the royal palace. This impressive building could seat 3,000 people in huge rooms, and it boasted beautiful gardens with fountains and pools. The Great Speaker led officials, including priests, army commanders, judges, tax collectors, market overseers, **scribes**, and spies. Many nobles (families descended from the first Aztec king) also served as royal advisors. Below the king, priests, and nobles, there were several less powerful groups in Aztec society.

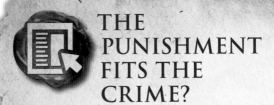

THE PUNISHMENT FITS THE CRIME?

All Aztec people had to obey strict laws. The **punishments** for breaking them could be very severe. The higher a person's rank, the worse the punishment. A judge or noble could be killed for being drunk in public, but an ordinary person might only have his home destroyed or his head shaved (a sign of shame) for a first offense.

This Aztec ruin found in Malinalco, Mexico, is just one example of the type of buildings the Aztec built. In contrast, the Royal Palace would be much larger.

This artist's drawing represents what an Aztec warrior may have looked like in full dress.

Aztec society was organized into *calpulli* (say "cal-pool-ee"), or clans, groups of related people who focused on a trade. These families were farmers, craftspeople, traveling merchants, and market traders. No one owned their own land—each clan owned the land together. Clans were responsible for members' good behavior and sometimes ran schools for their children. Rank and riches were usually decided by birth.

But a brave warrior could rise to become very respected. Eagle and Jaguar warriors were the cream of the crop. There were also many slaves—prisoners captured in battle, criminals, or poor people who had sold themselves to get money for food.

TEXT-DEPENDENT QUESTIONS

1. Explain the role of the Great Speaker.
2. Name one punishment the Aztecs carried out for breaking the law.
3. What were the Aztec clans called?

RESEARCH PROJECT

Some of the Aztec laws were very strict and could result in severe punishment. Research some of the punishments and crimes that existed in ancient Mexico. Compare them with some of the laws we have today. Would the Aztecs find our laws just as strange as we might find theirs? Prepare a presentation explaining some of the similarities and differences of the Aztec laws and today's laws.

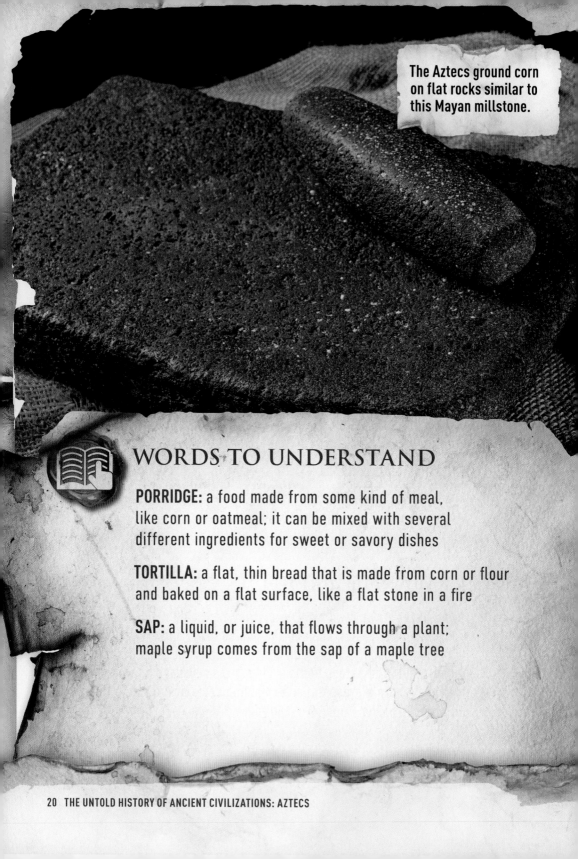

The Aztecs ground corn on flat rocks similar to this Mayan millstone.

WORDS TO UNDERSTAND

PORRIDGE: a food made from some kind of meal, like corn or oatmeal; it can be mixed with several different ingredients for sweet or savory dishes

TORTILLA: a flat, thin bread that is made from corn or flour and baked on a flat surface, like a flat stone in a fire

SAP: a liquid, or juice, that flows through a plant; maple syrup comes from the sap of a maple tree

CHAPTER 4

AUTHENTIC MEXICAN FOOD

E ver wonder where **tortillas** come from? The Aztecs made them hundreds of years ago out of sweet corn, or maize, one of their major crops. Aztec women ground dry corn on flat stones, making flour. They mixed the flour with water to make dough that they rolled out like cookie dough. To make them crispy, they would bake them on hot clay dishes. Or they would wrap them around a meat or vegetable mixture and steam them to make pancakes.

Aztec cooking included anything edible, including grasshoppers, which you still might find in modern Mexico.

The Aztecs used honey gathered from wild honeycomb like this one.

over Mexico City today that this was once a lake.

Learn some of the most fascinating facts of the Aztecs.

Aztec cooks, always women, also made **porridge** from maize grains or from the seeds of sage and other wild plants. For extra nourishment, and to add flavor, they served up almost anything edible they could find. Mostly, they made spicy vegetable stews, with chilies, tomatoes, beans, pumpkins, sweet potatoes, peppers, avocados, and boiled cactus leaves with the spines removed. Luxury foods included meat such as rabbit, deer, turkey,

WASTE NOT WANT NOT

The Aztecs brewed a strong alcoholic drink, called pulque (say "pul-kay"), from maguey cactus **sap**, or they'd boil it to make sticky syrup for sweetening food. They also found many strange uses for other parts of the plant. Its sharp spines were used like knives to draw blood in religious rituals. The pointed tips of its leaves could even be cut off and, with a long length of fiber attached, served as an instant needle and thread.

The prickly pear cactus was also put to good use as building material, glue, and medicine.

The Aztecs are still well-known for their spicy hot chocolate, or *xocolatl*. Look for the recipe at the end of this chapter

and hairless dog. But the Aztecs used everything—salamanders, grasshoppers, and even algae found their way onto the menu from time to time.

The Aztecs did not have cheese, milk, or butter. There were no cows, sheep, goats, or horses in Mesoamerica. They didn't have sugar either, but they did collect honey from wild bees.

They drank water or tea made with dried herbs and also brewed beer from chewed maize. Aztec kings, rich nobles, and merchants could afford a very special drink, called *xocolatl* (say "sho-kol-at-ull"), or chocolate made from crushed cacao beans, honey, and spices.

TEXT-DEPENDENT QUESTIONS

1. Where do tortillas come from?
2. Describe some of the food the Aztecs ate.
3. What is the name of a very special Aztec drink?

RESEARCH PROJECT

MAKE AN AZTEC-STYLE CHOCOLATE DRINK

People living in rainforests who had been conquered by the Aztecs sent them tributes of cacao beans. Today, we use these beans to make chocolate, but the Aztecs made them into a drink. They were so valuable that the Aztecs used them instead of money. They flavored their chocolate with another American rainforest plant, vanilla.

You will need (makes 2 servings):
- 2 mugs of milk
- 2 ¼ cups (100 g) chocolate (the darker the better) or 4 teaspoons pure cocoa powder
- 4 teaspoons honey (more if you like things very sweet)
- 2 drops vanilla essence
- cheese grater
- a saucepan

(Ask an adult to help you with this recipe.)

1. Grate the chocolate, or mix the cocoa powder with a little milk to make a smooth, runny paste.
2. Heat the milk in a saucepan.
3. When it is hot but NOT boiling, add the honey, grated chocolate or cocoa powder mix, and vanilla. Stir.
4. Keep on stirring until the honey and the chocolate or cocoa powder have dissolved.
5. Bring very gently to the boil, stirring all the time, then remove from the heat right away, and pour into two mugs.

OPTIONAL: For a spicy blend, add some cayenne chili powder to the drink.

The Aztecs valued family above all else.

WORDS TO UNDERSTAND

BRIDEGROOM: a newly married man or a man about to be married

HARSH: a hard or difficult situation or environment; something that is harsh is typically unpleasant

PRIVILEGE: a right or benefit for a person considered above other people in a group or society

CHAPTER 5

FAMILY VALUES

In the **harsh** place where the Aztecs lived, it would be impossible to survive without a family—the larger the better. Every person worked for the family business, whether it was farming or trading. They supported each other and looked after each other. If someone in the family broke a law, the whole family could be punished.

Old people, that is, anyone over fourty, called *ueuetque,* were respected for their knowledge and experience. They were given special **privileges** by Aztec laws. At wedding feasts, they were allowed to get drunk. Boys usually got married when they were about twenty years old, and girls when they were about sixteen. Marriages were arranged by match-makers or families. It was rude for a girl to say yes the first time she was asked!

GOOD LUCK FROM BAD NEWS

Childbirth was the most dangerous time in any married woman's life. In fact, Aztec women looked at giving birth like a battle. Although friends and midwives offered careful advice, such as "Don't go out at night for fear of evil spirits," many mothers died. A woman who died this way became "a companion of the Sun," just like a warrior. The Aztecs honored these dead women like gods or heroes and believed that their bodies had magic powers. Warriors tried to steal their hair or fingers as good-luck charms to hang on their shields.

This vase was made around 600 AD. You can learn to make your own pottery following these directions.

RESEARCH PROJECT

Follow along to make clay pots using the coil and pinch methods.

Materials:

- clay (earthenware, stoneware, modeling clay)
- sponge and water
- scoring tools (plastic butter knife, pencil, toothpicks, or wood modeling tools)
- wire clay cutter (optional)
- hard, flat building surface, such as a cutting board

Instructions:

Knead the Clay

1. Fold the clay in half, and press it with your palms using the weight of your body. Fold, press, and repeat.
2. If the clay becomes too dry, add a little water to soften it.
3. Continue to knead the clay until it feels bendy.
4. You can now make a pinch pot or coil pot.

Make a Coil Pot

1. Split the kneaded clay in half, and roll one of the halves into a ball.
2. Flatten the ball to form a base for your pot. You can use a wire clay cutter to remove it and set aside.
3. Divide the remaining clay into a few small pieces. Roll one piece into a coil, and score it.
4. Score the base, and add some water using a sponge. Attach the coil to the base, matching up the score marks.
5. Roll another small piece of clay into a coil, and attach it to the last coil, overlapping them slightly. Add as many coils as you like to build up the walls of the pot.
6. You can decorate your pot by making marks in the clay.
7. Once you finish, let your coil pot air dry.

Make a Pinch Pot

1. Roll all of the kneaded clay into a ball.
2. Use your thumb to push down into the center of the ball.
3. Use your thumb and fingers to pinch the clay from the center hole outwards, forming the walls of the pot.
4. You can decorate your pot by making marks in the clay.
5. Once you finish, let your pinch pot air dry.

This traditional costume is representative of what the Aztecs wore during special ceremonies.

An Aztec wedding was an important event, but it was based more on business or politics than love. The ceremony took place at night. The bride painted her face red or yellow and put on garlands of feathers and flowers. Then she was carried on the matchmaker's back to her **bridegroom's** parents' house. That would be her home for the rest of her life. Like most Aztec houses, it was small, plain, and simple, made of mud brick or soft stone, whitewashed, and thatched with reeds or cactus leaves. There was very little furniture, just a few mats, blankets, baskets, and clay cooking pots. The Aztecs did not have tables, chairs, beds, or metal tools.

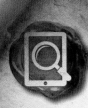

TEXT-DEPENDENT QUESTIONS

1. How old were boys and girls when they got married?
2. What was the most dangerous time in an Aztec woman's life?
3. Describe a traditional Aztec wedding.

These ruins in The Aztec Ruins National Monument in New Mexico, US, show a little bit of what an average Aztec house looked like.

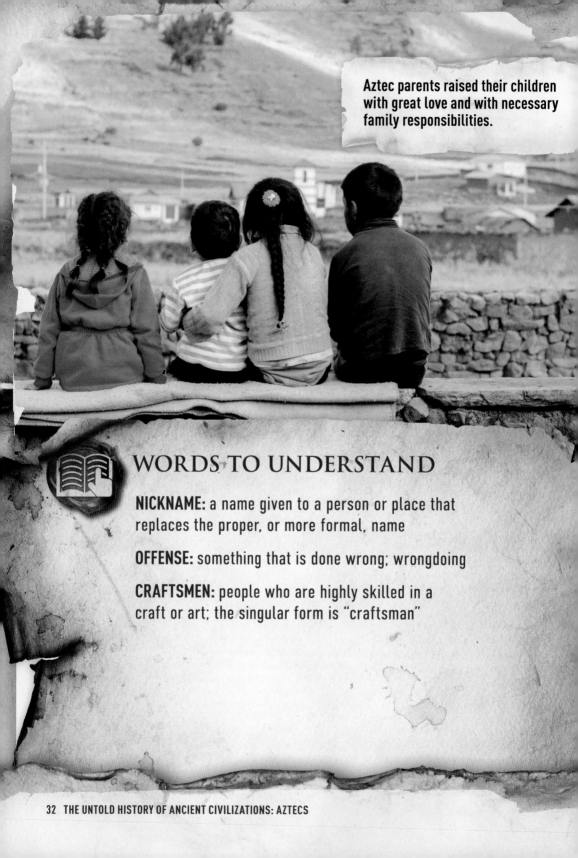

Aztec parents raised their children with great love and with necessary family responsibilities.

WORDS TO UNDERSTAND

NICKNAME: a name given to a person or place that replaces the proper, or more formal, name

OFFENSE: something that is done wrong; wrongdoing

CRAFTSMEN: people who are highly skilled in a craft or art; the singular form is "craftsman"

CHAPTER 6

A HAPPY CHILDHOOD

D o you have a **nickname** your parents or friends have given you? At the playground, you can hear "Sweetie" and "Honey." Aztec parents had names for their kids, too, such as "Precious Feather" or "Jewel."

Just like today, strict Aztec laws meant that a father could be punished if he did not support his family.

Newborn babies were welcomed into the world with cries of joy. Family members ran around, shouting the new baby's name.

Children were named after the day and month they were born, so some Aztec people had names we might think strange today, such as Seven Rabbit or Three Wind (the months were numbered one to thirteen, and the days had names like Rabbit and Lizard). Children had personal names as well, such as Angry Turkey or Turquoise Flower.

SCHOOL AND CHORES

Children had to help around the home. By the time they were four, boys were expected to fetch water and carry firewood. When they were six, they began to learn how to work in the fields. Girls age twelve were taught cooking, and boys age thirteen were taught how to paddle and steer a canoe.

Boys and girls, men and women had different roles in the Aztec culture and traditions.

As they grew up, boys and girls were taught to be respectful, obedient, and cheerful. Aztec children enjoyed lots of toys and games, and teenage girls sometimes challenged local boys to pillow fights. But if children were rude or lazy, their parents could punish them. They might be shut outside overnight or pricked with cactus spikes. For more serious **offenses**, the child could be held over burning chili pepper. The smoke could burn their eyes and lips.

Girls stayed at home and were taught household skills by their mothers, although girls from noble families could become priestesses. Boys from ordinary families learned to be **craftsmen**, laborers, or farmers. At fifteen, most boys went to local schools to learn to be warriors. Boys from rich or noble families, and those who were especially gifted, might train to be priests or scribes. They studied history, astronomy, and poetry and were taught how to read and write.

Many Aztec traditions are still practiced today in Mexico such as this shaman blessing this baby in Mexico City.

TEXT-DEPENDENT QUESTIONS

1. What are some of the common names Aztec children were given?
2. What were some different roles between Aztec boys and girls?
3. What did Aztec children do when they grew up?

RESEARCH PROJECT

Children from different cultures are raised in many different ways. Research some of the differences between how children are raised in your culture and how they are raised in other cultures. What are the similarities? What are the differences? Create a chart showing these similarities and differences. Ask your teacher if you can present your chart in class.

This illustration depicts the traditional male clothing of the Aztecs.

WORDS TO UNDERSTAND

FIBER: a fine, threadlike piece of something; the Aztecs made things out of cactus fiber

LOOM: a tool that weaves fabric; the Aztecs used this to make clothing

RANK: a position in a society or profession

CHAPTER 7

THE AZTEC LOOK

A ztecs had many of the same jobs we have today. But there was no such thing as an Aztec fashion model. Everyone wore the same thing, no matter their age or **rank**. There was one basic design for men and one for women. Men and boys wore a loincloth and a short blanket tied at one shoulder to make a cloak. Women and girls wore a loose blouse and an ankle-length skirt.

This illustration shows the traditional female clothing of the Aztecs.

The headdress seen here was typically worn by noble men and women.

By law, ordinary people's clothes had to be made of plain material. Usually this was made of cactus **fiber.** It was rough and coarse but not prickly. Slaves might wear nothing but a loincloth. Nobles might have finer, smoother cloth woven from cotton and decorated with brightly colored embroidery. It was a serious crime for an ordinary person to dress in nobles' clothes. If found out, the person might be executed.

From this video, you'll discover just what it takes to be a Jaguar Warrior.

Noblewomen and noblemen were also allowed to wear jewelry and headdresses made with the beautiful feathers of rare rainforest birds. They could also carry fans and flowers. Aztec jewelry was carefully made by hand from pure gold, precious stones, coral, pearls, and jade.

EXPRESSING YOURSELF

Cloth was woven by women and girls using backstrap **looms**. These were light and portable and could be used almost anywhere. Aztec weavers used this simple technology to create very complicated patterns based on shells, jewels, fish, monsters, jaguars, and butterflies. Sometimes they wove rabbit fur or feathers into the fabric.

The traditional Aztec culture is still celebrated in Mexico during celebrations.

By looking at an Aztec's hairstyle, you could often tell their age, clan, and job. Young girls wore their hair long and loose. Young men who had not yet killed an enemy in battle did so as well. They had to leave some of their hair uncut to show that they were not yet "real men." Married women braided their hair and arranged it in two horns on top of their heads. Adult warriors cut their hair at about ear length and tied some of it up in a topknot. And priests kept their hair long.

TEXT-DEPENDENT QUESTIONS

1. In day-to-day life, what did Aztec men and women wear?
2. What were noblemen and noblewomen allowed to wear?
3. Some Aztec men and women wore their hair in different styles for different reasons. What were some of these styles and reasons?

RESEARCH PROJECT

MAKE A FEATHER HEADDRESS

Aztec people wore wonderful headdresses made of brightly colored feathers from tropical birds. The bigger the headdress, the more important the wearer!

You will need:

Sheets of colored paper; a pen or pencil; scissors; a wide plastic headband or a piece of ribbon about 1 in. (2.5 cm) wide, long enough to fit comfortably around your head with enough left over to tie in a bow; some plastic "jewels" or gold-colored paper; glue suitable to use on fabric.

1. Draw feather shapes (at least 20), about 8 in. (20 cm) long, on colored paper. Cut them out and cut fringes at the top end of each one.

2. Stick the feathers onto your headband or ribbon.

3. Decorate the feathers with plastic jewels or shapes cut from gold paper.

4. Put on your headband, or tie the ribbon under your chin.

There are codex pictures of Aztecs wearing headdresses. The feathers did not stand up vertically but stuck out backwards behind the wearer's head. You can do a search online to see examples of the headdresses.

Similar to these Mayan etchings, the Aztecs carved images of their gods on rock buildings.

WORDS TO UNDERSTAND

DESCENDANTS: family members; offspring of a person; your children would be considered your descendants

ELABORATE: something that is highly decorated or fancy

HAUNT: a visit from a ghost or spirit; or to visit a place often

CHAPTER 8

THE POWER
OF PRAYER

Just as their gods brought them to their land, so did these gods shape the Aztecs' everyday lives. Today some people pray every morning or evening, and the Aztecs talked to their gods too. The first thing every day, Aztec men, women, and children pricked their ears and offered two drops of blood to the gods to give thanks for still being alive.

Tlaloc, the Aztec god of rain, is just one example of the gods the Aztecs worshipped.

Can you see the ring on the side of the rock wall? This is the hoop Aztecs used to play their game.

Aztecs believed that their fate and the fate of the world depended on hundreds of gods. Each one had different powers—some were friendly, but others were frightening. Some were the spirits of dead rulers who guided their **descendants**. Some were ancient nature gods, honored by all Mesoamerican peoples. Some, like Huitzilopochtli, or God of the Sun, belonged to the Aztecs alone. But a few Aztecs preferred to worship just one supreme god. They called him Tloque Nahuaque (say "tlow-kay nah-hwah-kay"), or Lord of Nowhere, because he was everywhere.

Magic was part of everyday life for the Aztecs. Gods could be kind, but the witches, ghosts, and demons that **haunted** the night were all very dangerous. They appeared as skulls that chased passers-by as spooky miniature women or as headless and footless creatures who moaned and rolled on the ground. Monsters called *tzitzimime* (say "tsee-tsee-mee-may") who wore necklaces and headdresses of cut-off human hands also lay in wait, ready to pounce on their victims.

The Aztecs honored their gods and kept ghosts and demons at bay by holding **elaborate** festivals. Some were violent and terrifying. Others were more cheerful, with music, singing and dancing in the streets, feasting, and ritual games. The largest, but one of the rarest, Aztec festival was Xiuhmolpilli, which meant "new fire." It was held once every fifty-two years to prevent the end of the world.

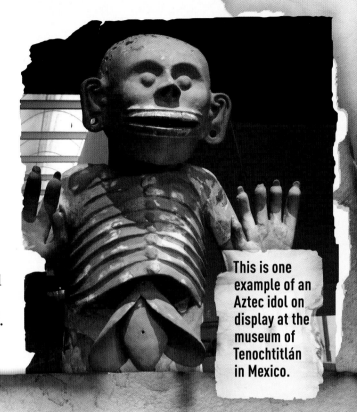

This is one example of an Aztec idol on display at the museum of Tenochtitlán in Mexico.

TEXT-DEPENDENT QUESTIONS

1. What was another name for the Aztec God of Sun?
2. Other than gods, what other kinds of creatures did the Aztecs believe in?
3. Why did the Aztecs hold so many rituals?

RESEARCH PROJECT

The Aztecs were not the only civilization to have several gods. Can you find what other cultures and civilizations worship many gods—either today or in the past? Try an Internet search, and create a short presentation explaining the gods worshipped in several different cultures.

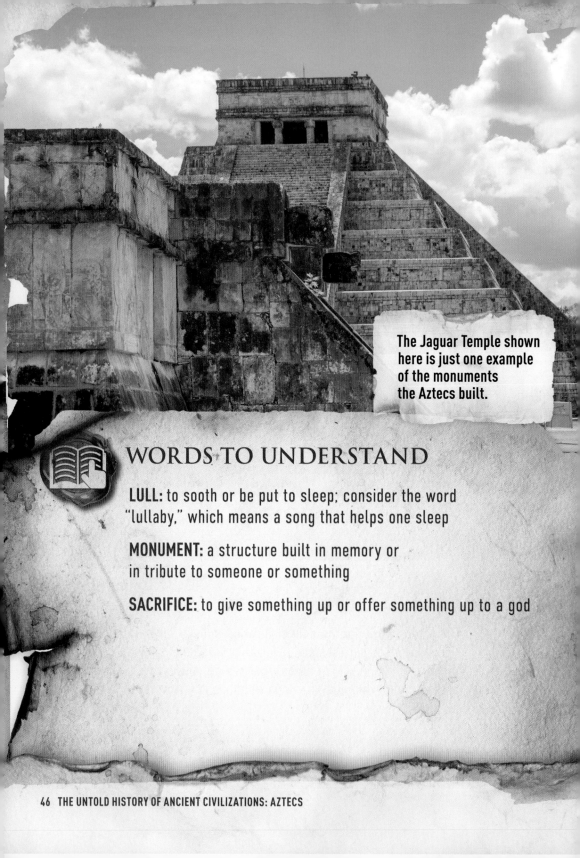

The Jaguar Temple shown
here is just one example
of the monuments
the Aztecs built.

WORDS TO UNDERSTAND

LULL: to sooth or be put to sleep; consider the word
"lullaby," which means a song that helps one sleep

MONUMENT: a structure built in memory or
in tribute to someone or something

SACRIFICE: to give something up or offer something up to a god

CHAPTER 9

SYMBOLS OF PRIDE

All throughout time, people have built **monuments** to their gods, and the Aztecs were no different. Their technical know-how allowed them to build the Great Temple, which towered almost 90 ft. (30 m) high in the center of Tenochtitlán. It was a symbol of Aztec pride. Inside were statues of Huitzilopochtli, the Aztecs' own special god, and Tlaloc, the god of rain.

Temples began as pyramid-shaped mounds made of earth, stones, and cement. They grew taller over the years as each new king added an extra layer or built a new shrine (holy room) on top of the mound. Perhaps the best-known Aztec pyramid today is the Great Pyramid, or Temple Mayor, at 197 ft. (600 m) tall.

Shrines were reached by danger-ously steep steps, often too small to put a whole foot on. Priests kept constant vigil there, offering flowers, incense, and prayers. They also drummed, chanted, and made human **sacrifices** to the gods.

HUNGRY GODS

No one wants to volunteer to be sacrificed—or do they? Aztec priests and poets taught that it was an honor to be sacrificed. There are few reports of victims protesting. But they may have been drugged or **lulled** into a trance by the priests' chanting and drumming. Or they may have agreed to die in the hope of a good life in the next world. Scientists think the Aztecs may have sacrificed thousands of people each year.

The famous Temple Mayor is 197 ft. (600 m) tall.

The Aztecs believed that they must feed the gods with blood, human hearts, or human tears, or the world would come to an end. Most of those killed were criminals and prisoners captured in war. Special sacrificial stones stood at the top of temple steps where priests killed victims with sharp flint knives and cut their hearts out. *Chac-mool* containers—shaped like water gods—were placed nearby to hold the hearts, while blood poured down the temple steps.

This chac-mool is in the ancient ruins of Tula de Allende in Hidalgo, Mexico.

The ideal victim was young, fit, handsome, and preferably, male. The Aztecs thought they should only give the best to the gods. Priests also drowned Aztec children in springtime to encourage the rain to fall and beheaded young girls (the same height as the tall maize plants) when the first maize cobs were ready to harvest in the hope it would guarantee good crops.

The Aztec relied heavily on maize crops, so they did what they thought was best to ensure a healthy harvest.

TEXT-DEPENDENT QUESTIONS

1. What is the most famous Aztec-built pyramid?
2. Why did the Aztecs sacrifice people?
3. Describe a chac-mool and its use.

RESEARCH PROJECT

Many religions expect some kind of sacrifice. Research the kinds of sacrifices used in religions across the world. Make a chart of their differences and similarities.

A basket of cacao beans was just one example of taxes the Aztec collected from the people they ruled.

WORDS TO UNDERSTAND

AMBASSADOR: a person of high rank sent from one civilization to represent another civilization

JADE: a highly valuable stone that is often green; it was used in Aztec culture for making jewelry

REIGN: the period of time in which a leader, or king, rules

CHAPTER 10

AZTEC CONQUERORS

The Aztecs did not move into the land that is now Mexico peacefully. The people who were already there fought back. Then, to support their growing population they needed more resources. And the only way to get what they needed was to take them from others.

Eventually, they took control of the city-states all around them. They sent armies to invade or **ambassadors** to threaten an attack. Usually city leaders surrendered, and the Aztec empire grew rapidly after around AD 1400. Aztec armies did not destroy the cities they conquered. Instead, they collected tributes (taxes) from them twice a year. They demanded to be given valuable items, such as feathers, baskets of chilies, necklaces, lip plugs, jaguar skins, **jade** and turquoise, gold dust and cacao beans.

TAKING CARE OF PRISONERS

Strangely, the Aztecs did not aim to kill their opponents in battle. Instead, they hoped to capture them alive and take them back to their temples to be sacrificed to the gods. While an enemy prisoner was still alive, the Aztec who captured him was supposed to treat him kindly, like a father, and feed him well.

This totem water fountain demonstrates the importance religion had on the Aztec culture.

Each new Aztec king had to start his **reign** with a battle. It was his duty to seek fame and glory and to take prisoners for sacrifice. All Aztec men also had a duty to fight. Spears, bows, and arrows were the Aztecs' favorite weapons, but they also carried deadly war clubs made of stone and tipped with razor-sharp flakes of obsidian (volcanic glass). These could cut an enemy's head off. Top warriors went to war dressed in birds' feathers or animal skins. They hoped the skins would protect them, and they would gain some of the eagle's or jaguar's courage and strength.

In one "war," however, there were no casualties. In times of peace, the Aztecs and their neighbors would have a War of the Flowers. This war was more like a tournament, where each side would take prisoners. When one side captured enough prisoners, the battle was ended, and everyone returned home.

Headdresses adorned with eagle or jaguar heads were reserved for the most courageous warriors.

TEXT-DEPENDENT QUESTIONS

1. When did the Aztec empire begin to grow rapidly?
2. Why did the Aztec empire begin to grow?
3. What is the importance of the eagle and jaguar in Aztec culture?

RESEARCH PROJECT

The text discusses a War of the Flowers. Research more on this, and create a presentation depicting the events of this "war."

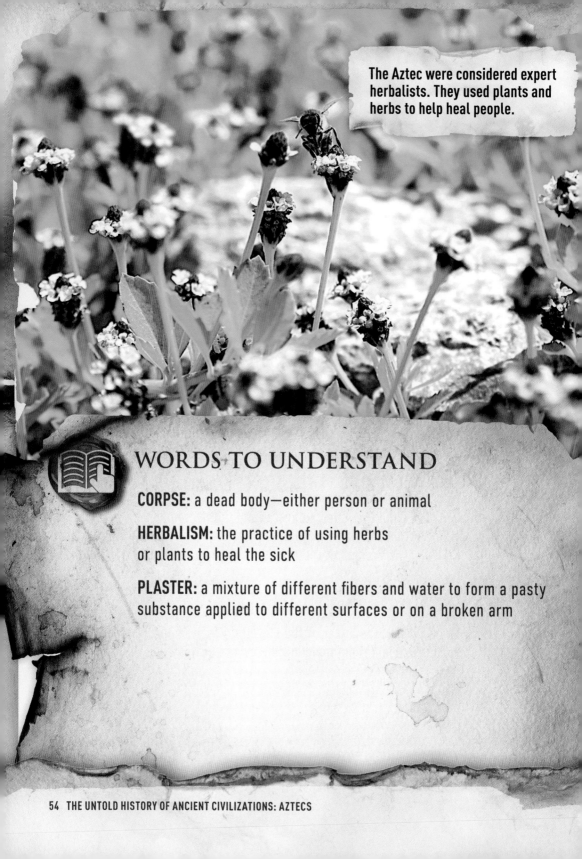

The Aztec were considered expert herbalists. They used plants and herbs to help heal people.

WORDS TO UNDERSTAND

CORPSE: a dead body—either person or animal

HERBALISM: the practice of using herbs or plants to heal the sick

PLASTER: a mixture of different fibers and water to form a pasty substance applied to different surfaces or on a broken arm

CHAPTER 11

A SHORT LIFE

L ife as an Aztec was not easy. Many children died before the age of five. Those who lived longer faced the dangers of illness, war, long journeys, and even sacrifice. Older Aztecs enjoyed special privileges. But most men and women died before they were fifty.

Aztec medicine was a mixture of religion, **herbalism**, magic, and first aid. They believed prevention was the best form of medicine. However, doctors could set broken limbs expertly in **plaster**, clean wounds with urine (strangely, this was safer than dirty water), say prayers, and recite magic spells. They grew herbs and medicinal plants in gardens and collected seeds and berries from wild rainforests. Some Aztec treatments worked, but others were very dangerous.

The bodies of important Aztecs were buried in tombs. They were dressed in fine clothes, and all their treasures were buried with them together with a pet dog for company. If they were male, and really powerful, some of their wives and servants might be killed and buried, too.

Ordinary people's **corpses** were wrapped in cloth to make a mummy bundle. This was decorated with paper ornaments and feathers, and a mask was placed over its face. Then the whole bundle was burned.

THE END OF THE WORLD

The Aztecs' worst fear was that the world would come to an end. They believed it had been destroyed four times before, by jaguars, wind, fire, and water. Each time, it had been born again. But now they lived in the fifth, and final, world. If it ended, there would be nothing to follow.

This image shows some of the items unearthed in Aztec tombs.

The Aztecs could have covered the dead with masks like this one.

Most Aztecs feared a miserable future after death. They believed they would work for the gods in the afterlife. The job you ended up with depended on what you did during your life on Earth. The Wind of Knives would cut the flesh from their bones, and they would spend four years on a dangerous journey, chased by monsters, until they reached *Mictlan* (say "meek-tlan")— hell. Then they would disappear. But warriors, mothers who died in child-birth, and human sacrifices would be reborn.

This video explains what happened to the Aztecs.

TEXT-DEPENDENT QUESTIONS

1. How did the Aztecs help heal sick people?
2. Where did the Aztecs bury important people?
3. What did the Aztec people fear most?

RESEARCH PROJECT

Many common plants and herbs have healing properties, such as the dandelion, which is considered a good use to treat minor infections. Consult an expert about other common medicinal plants and write a two- to three-page report about your discoveries. WARNING: Some plants and herbs can make you very sick. Make sure not to eat any plant that you're unsure of. Always consult an expert before tasting any wild plant.

AZTEC FACTS

SIMPLE TECHNOLOGY: The Aztecs had no iron, no roads, no horses, no big machines, and no wheeled transport, although they did make wheeled toys.

MONEY BEANS: There were no coins or paper money in Aztec lands. Instead, the Aztecs bartered (exchanged) goods of equal value and used cacao beans or quills filled with gold dust as money.

NO RECOGNITION: Aztec artists and crafts-people did not sign their work. They believed their skills were a gift from the gods, so they did not deserve individual praise.

BARK BOOKS: Only specially trained scribes could read and write. A scribe, called a *tlacuilo* (say "tlah-kweel-oh"), meaning "thought writer," would use picture writing to record Aztec history, myths, and astronomy. Aztec books, called codices, were made of long, folded strips of fig tree bark or deerskin.

THE GOD WHO DIED: Like many other Mesoamericans, the Aztecs worshipped Quetzalcoatl, or Feathered Serpent, an ancient god king. They believed he had sacrificed himself to help the people he ruled. Legends told how, one day, he would return to Mexico. Soon afterward, the world would end.

THE END OF THE WORLD—FOR THE AZTECS: Cortés made friends with the Aztecs' enemies, and together they marched on Tenochtitlán. In 1521, Cortés and his soldiers set fire to the city and killed three quarters of its people. Aztec power ended in 1524, when the last Aztec king died. In 1535, Mexico was made a colony, ruled by Spain, and many Spanish people migrated to live there.

AZTECS TODAY: People descended from the Aztecs still live in Mexico today. They speak Nahuatl, the Aztec language, eat favorite Aztec foods, and sometimes wear clothes with Aztec designs. Many Aztec customs also survive, mingled with Christian traditions. For example, on the Day of the Dead, Mexican families bring flowers and sweets shaped like Aztec-style skulls to their ancestors' graves.

MEN OR MONSTERS? In 1519, Spanish nobleman Hernán Cortés landed in Mexico with a troop of soldiers. They were searching for gold. The Aztecs had never seen European men before and were alarmed by their hairy chests and bushy beards. They thought that the new arrivals might be Quetzalcoatl or other strange, feathered gods. They also were puzzled by European sailing ships, which looked like huge houses floating on the water and by men riding on horseback. To the Aztecs, they seemed to be monsters, half human and half beast.

SIGNS FROM THE GODS? Shortly before Hernán Cortés and the Spanish landed, priests reported many strange omens. These included a temple catching fire, a tidal wave, and weird, bodiless voices wailing in the streets at night.

FURTHER RESOURCES

FURTHER READING

Ganeri, Anita. *How the Aztecs Lived.* New York: Gareth Stevens, 2011.

Green, Jen. *Hail! Aztecs.* New York: Crabtree Pub., 2011.

Powell, Jillian. *The Gruesome Truth About the Aztecs.* New York: Windmill Books, 2011.

Raum, Elizabeth. *What Did the Aztecs Do for Me?* Chicago, IL: Heinemann Library, 2011.

Sayer, Cloë. *Aztecs and Incas.* Mankato, MN: Stargazer Books, 2010.

INTERNET RESOURCES

Find out more about the Aztecs from these websites. Remember the Internet is constantly changing, so if you can't find these websites, try searching using the word "Aztecs."

The Awesome Aztecs
http://aztecs.mrdonn.org/

Aztecs, Maya, and Inca
http://www.ducksters.com/history/aztec_maya_inca.php

Mexicolore
http://www.ducksters.com/history/aztec_maya_inca.php

Kids Discover
http://www.kidsdiscover.com/shop/issues/aztecs-for-kids/

EDUCATIONAL VIDEO LINKS

Aztecs1: Examine the Aztecs' impressive system of aqueducts that supplied water for irrigation and bathing. http://x-qr.net/1DMc

Aztecs2: Learn some of the most fascinating facts of the Aztecs. http://x-qr.net/1HAS

Aztecs3: From this video, you'll discover just what it takes to be a Jaguar Warrior. http://x-qr.net/1EdY

Aztecs4: This video explains what happened to the Aztecs. http://x-qr.net/1Hbi

PHOTO CREDITS

INDEX